S0-ARY-350

CONCORD SOUTH SIDE SCHOOL

The Picture Life of
ELIZABETH II

Queen Elizabeth's personal flag. The initial E, the crown, and the chaplet of roses are in gold on a blue field. The flag is flown when the Queen is present in person or from buildings where she is residing.

THE PICTURE LIFE OF

ELIZABETH II

BY DOUGLAS LIVERSIDGE

Illustrated with Photographs

FRANKLIN WATTS, INC.
575 Lexington Avenue
New York, N.Y. 10022

Cover photograph:

H. M. Queen Elizabeth II in the White Drawing Room at Buckingham Palace. She is wearing the Sash and Star of the Order of the Garter with Family Orders on the shoulder.

Photo by Anthony Buckley

Copyright © 1969 by Franklin Watts, Inc.
Library of Congress Catalog Card Number: 69-16982
Printed in the United States of America
by The Moffa Press, Inc.
1 2 3 4 5

The Picture Life of
ELIZABETH II

Her title is Her Majesty Queen Elizabeth II of the United Kingdom of Great Britain and Northern Ireland and her other realms and territories, Head of the Commonwealth, Defender of the Faith. She is known to hundreds of millions of people throughout the world. Her picture appears every day on millions of stamps, coins, currency, and documents, not only of the United Kingdom and its dependencies but also of the Commonwealth countries, former British territories which are now fully independent and govern themselves.

The Imperial State Crown, a symbol of the monarchy, was worn by the Queen leaving Westminster Abbey after her coronation. The crown is worn on all state occasions.

A country ruled by a king or queen is called a monarchy. Today the British have a democratic form of government and the monarch, or head of state, has much less actual power than in the past. Unlike the representatives to Parliament, the monarch is not elected by a vote of the people. Succession to the throne is determined by order of birth. In the United Kingdom the title of monarch goes from parent to child. If a king or queen has one or more sons, the eldest son becomes the ruler when his parent dies.

Princess Elizabeth (standing) with her sister, Princess Margaret, and her parents, formerly the Duke and Duchess of York, and eventually King George VI and Queen Elizabeth.

Queen Elizabeth's descent goes back to Egbert, a king who united all the English in 829. Her father, George VI, had two children, both girls. Since he had no sons, Elizabeth, his elder daughter, became queen after his death. She herself has three sons, so the next monarch of the United Kingdom will be a man.

She is constitutional head of the government of the United Kingdom and head of the royal family.

The Garter King of Arms in the presence of other officers of the College of Heralds, at St. James's Palace, London, on February 8, 1952, proclaims Princess Elizabeth Queen Elizabeth II.

Although the United Kingdom is a
   democracy, authority throughout the
   country is traced back to Queen Elizabeth.
She has the power to conclude treaties, to
   cede or accept territories, to declare war,
   and to make peace, although she would do
   so only on Cabinet advice.

As constitutional head of the government, she acts on the advice of her Ministers. Parliament makes laws. When signed by the Queen, they are official. She chooses the Prime Minister. This usually is a matter of approving the head of the party which has the most votes in the House of Commons.

Arriving for the State Opening of Parliament.

With Prince Philip at her side, Her Majesty reads the Speech in the House of Lords.

She opens each session of Parliament with a speech which, written for her by her Ministers, explains the government's future policies.

At least once a week the Prime Minister informs the Queen of all important matters. Over the years the Queen has accumulated a lot of knowledge of state affairs and can be very helpful with advice. This advice does not have to be taken by the Prime Minister, but it is listened to carefully.

The power of the courts also stems from the Queen. She appoints judges and can pardon or show mercy to the convicted. In fact, wrongdoing is punished as a breach of "the Queen's peace." As "the fountain of honour," she confers peerages, knighthoods, and other honours. The orders in the Queen's personal gifts are the Garter, the Thistle, the Victorian Order, and the Order of Merit. All other honours are given on the recommendation of the Prime Minister. She appoints the leading clergymen of the Established Church of England. Prayers are said for her and the royal family at the services of the Church.

She is the constitutional as well as the ceremonial head of the government, which, in the United Kingdom, is called Her Majesty's Government.

The monarchy is associated with many customs and ceremonies. Each June the Queen makes the traditional drive along the course at the Ascot race meeting.

As the nation's chief hostess, she entertains
visiting heads of state, and receives the
credentials of foreign ambassadors who
arrive at her court, the Court of St. James.
She travels at times to other countries and
is welcomed as the representative of her
people.

During a state visit to Britain, the President of Chile (center) gave a luncheon party in honour of the Queen.

The Queen in an elephant procession in Benares during her royal tour of India.

As a girl, Queen Elizabeth never went to a regular school. Special tutors instructed her in constitutional, political, and economic affairs, and all the other subjects that would be essential to her as queen. Her children are getting a more formal education. From school Prince Charles went to Cambridge University.

On November 20, 1947, she married Prince Philip of Greece. At the time, she was Princess Elizabeth, since her father was still king. Prince Philip was known as Lieutenant Philip Mountbatten. His present title is His Royal Highness, The Prince Philip, Duke of Edinburgh.

On November 20, 1947, Princess Elizabeth married Prince Philip at Westminster Abbey.

Because her father was in ill health, Princess Elizabeth helped him with his royal duties. With Prince Philip, she embarked early in 1952 on an official tour of Kenya, Ceylon, Australia, and New Zealand. In February, while spending the night in an African treetop hotel watching wild beasts drink at a jungle pool, she learned her father had died on February 6. She became queen at the moment her father died.

Princess Elizabeth helped her father with his royal duties. She gave a banquet in honour of President Truman at the Canadian Embassy in Washington, D.C., on November 1, 1951.

On June 2, 1953, she was crowned at Westminster Abbey.

The Archbishop of Canterbury raising St. Edward's Crown before placing it on the Queen's head.

A dog lover, the Queen leads Wren, one of her black Labrador retrievers, during dog trials near her private home at Balmoral.

Queen Elizabeth has three official residences: Buckingham Palace, Windsor Castle beside the River Thames in Berkshire, and the Palace of Holyroodhouse in Edinburgh. In addition, she has private homes at Balmoral, where, during each summer vacation, she can roam with her children about the Scottish countryside; and at the Sandringham estate, Norfolk, where by tradition the royal family gathers during the Christmas vacation.

Most of the Queen's days are spent in London at Buckingham Palace. Each morning she goes to her study on the first floor of the north wing of the palace. There she reads the immense flow of official papers — many of which must be signed — and the dispatches from the Foreign Office. Since she is the servant of the people, anyone can write to her. Thus much mail arrives at the Palace Post Office. Her page sorts the letters, many of which are opened and read by the Queen herself.

At this desk in her study at Buckingham Palace, the Queen attends to affairs of state.

350 Acq ROBERTS

CONCORD SOUTH SIDE SCHOOL

25

There are also the daily audiences. And because the Queen in her person represents the state, she must take part in the nation's life by making public appearances. This burden is shared by other members of the royal family. By keeping a wall map in the palace, showing when and

Public visits form part of the Queen's activities. Here she receives a bouquet from two young members of the Commonwealth as she opens the Commonwealth Buildings of the Post-Graduate Medical School at Hammersmith Hospital, London.

where each visit is made, Queen Elizabeth maintains a custom begun by her father. During the Second World War, in one three-year period, royal visits totaled over three thousand, an achievement that inspired the King to remark, "We are not a family; we are a firm."

Princess Margaret tries out equipment in a new language laboratory for partially blind girls at Chorleywood College.

Queen Elizabeth, with Prince Philip, receiving members of the cast of the Munich National Theatre.

One interest of the Court is its traditional patronage of the arts and sciences. Thus the prefix "royal" appears in the name of many distinguished societies. Artists, for instance, submit their pictures to the Royal Academy, and eminent scientists are Fellows of the Royal Society. The royal family are patrons not only of learning, but of the entertainment world, of sport, and of many voluntary organizations.

Every year the Queen appears at many
public events, and her picture is shown in
newspapers and on television screens in
many lands. Her Christmas broadcast is
heard all over the globe.

Queen Elizabeth, in 1952, making her first Christmas Day broadcast to listeners all over the world.

Another of Queen Elizabeth's duties is being the wife of Prince Philip and the mother of four children. When she is in London, she spends at least one hour daily without interruption with her children, no matter how many other duties she has. Her children are Charles, Prince of Wales, the eldest, who will on the death of his mother become king, Princess Anne, and Princes Andrew and Edward.

Queen Elizabeth with her family in the grounds of Frogmore, a house in Home Park, Windsor. Prince Philip is followed by Princess Anne. Behind the Queen are Charles, Prince of Wales (heir to the throne), Prince Andrew, and Prince Edward.

Each June the Queen takes the salute at the traditional Trooping the Colour ceremony. This event began so that each man would recognize his flag in battle. Now this historical event is carried out to mark the sovereign's official birthday.

Today the British people see the royal family as more of a family than they did in the past. In Queen Elizabeth's family they see their ideal of family life and, in a sense, a reflection of themselves. And because of her long ancestral line, the Queen is to the people the living representative of a history stretching into the remote past.

The Order of the Garter, which dates from 1348, is Britain's oldest Order of Chivalry. Here, the Queen walks with Prince Philip in the procession at Windsor Castle for the Order of the Garter service.

HER MAJESTY QUEEN ELIZABETH II

Born: 17, Bruton Street, London, W.1., April 21, 1926.
             Elder daughter of the Duke and Duchess of
             York (later King George VI and Queen Eliza-
             beth); sister, Her Royal Highness Princess
             Margaret.

Education: Private tutors at Buckingham Palace.

Family: Husband, His Royal Highness, The Prince
             Philip, Duke of Edinburgh; married Novem-
             ber 20, 1947. Children, H.R.H. Prince Charles,
             Prince of Wales (heir to the throne), H.R.H.
             Princess Anne, H.R.H. Prince Andrew, H.R.H.
             Prince Edward.